Samba HANON

MUSICIANS INSTITUTE

50 Exercises for the Beginning to Professional Pianist

By Peter Deneff

ISBN-13: 978-1-4234-1327-1
ISBN-10: 1-4234-1327-X

HAL•LEONARD®
CORPORATION

7777 W. BLUEMOUND RD. P.O. BOX 13819 MILWAUKEE, WI 53213

In Australia Contact:
Hal Leonard Australia Pty. Ltd.
4 Lentara Court
Cheltenham, Victoria, 3192 Australia
Email: ausadmin@halleonard.com

Visit Hal Leonard Online at
www.halleonard.com

for
George V. Deneff

About the author

Peter Deneff grew up in Long Beach, California listening to Greek and classical music and studying classical piano with Leaine Gibson. After starting his professional life playing in a Greek wedding band at age fifteen, he became obsessed with straight-ahead and Latin jazz. He began jazz studies with renowned pianist Mike Garson, where he crafted his art through studying some of the great jazz improvisers such as Charlie Parker, Bud Powell, and Chick Corea. During this time he also studied many ethnic styles that eventually led to the development of his classical and jazz compositional style as well as the formation of his Middle Eastern-Latin jazz group Excursion *(www.excursionjazz.com)*. He also pursued undergraduate and graduate studies in classical composition and film scoring at California State University Long Beach under the direction of Dr. Justus Matthews, Dr. Martin Herman and Perry Lamarca. Peter has written several best-selling books for Hal Leonard Corporation including *Jazz Hanon, Blues Hanon*, and *Salsa Hanon*. He has also composed and performed music for the Charles Sheen film, *Five Aces*. Deneff has performed at such varied venues as the Greek Theater, the Carpenter Performing Arts Center, the Playboy Jazz Festival, the Los Angeles Street Scene, the Orange County Street Fair, Universal Studios, the NAMM show, and the Baked Potato. His stylistic versatility has allowed him to play and/or sing with a diverse assortment of groups like Tierra, Ike Willis (singer with Frank Zappa), the Leslie Paula/Universal Studios Salsa Band, and Ebi, a notable Persian singer. Deneff also continues to play and record modern and folk Greek music for numerous events (www.synthesimusic.com) as well as an occasional Middle Eastern or jazz gig. Besides performing, Peter has also taught in many institutions such as Musician's Institute, Orange County High School of the Arts, and Cypress College, where he continues to teach classical and jazz piano. He spends most of his time in his studio producing projects for Yamaha Corporation *(Disklavier, Clavinova, Internet Direct Content)* and Hal Leonard Corporation *(PVG Play-Alongs, MI Press-Hanon Series)*.

Introduction

The genre of music generally known as "Latin" contains within it a myriad of sub-styles which include salsa, samba, reggae, ska, son, mariachi, and calypso. However, the two musical worlds which are most often misunderstood and mistakenly combined are the musical cultures of Brazil and Cuba. It is true that these two cultures contain common African elements and origins, but it is in the application of these musical materials that the two styles diverge. Whereas *Salsa Hanon* deals with the technical difficulties of playing the syncopated piano montunos of Cuban music, this book deals with the more subtle syncopations and voicings of Brazilian samba, bossa nova, Afro-Brazilian axé, and Brazilian jazz.

The approach taken with this book is a bit of a digression from the other books in this series. Instead of the exercises progressing in a sequential and repetitive manner, generally increasing in difficulty, these etudes can be practiced in any order. The student can pick and choose which studies they want to play and in which order they want to play them. There is more variance between the exercises and they tend to avoid a repetitive structure. Some of them are based on chromatic successions; others are actual chord progression that one might find in a typical samba. The student is encouraged to practice these studies with a sequenced drum pattern or midi sequencer and generally have fun with them. They may be played as fast as the player is able, but the tempo guidelines are 60-120 BPM.

The student should expect to become proficient at comping and playing riffs over samba rhythms. They will also become more comfortable with the technique of playing over a forward or reverse clave or beat emphasis. Through the varied exercises contained herein, the player will learn to play idiomatic piano ostinatos that would be heard in the music of Antonio Carlos Jobim, João Gilberto, Astrud Gilberto, Luiz Bonfá, and Sergio Mendes.

As always, some pointers one should keep in mind while practicing are:
- Back should be straight with shoulders relaxed.
- Hands should be low profile with fingers curved.
- Always practice with a metronome.
- Tempo should be as fast as the exercise can be performed accurately.
- Playing should be clean and even.
- Don't forget to breathe!

If one practices these studies with consistency, the physical requirements of samba, bossa, and even some jazz styles will be more easily overcome. Of course, as in all disciplines, the student must enjoy the process as well as the results in order to be successful. So relax and enjoy practicing, learning, and attaining new levels of proficiency as you navigate your lifelong journey of musical development.

Happy playing!

Peter Deneff

1

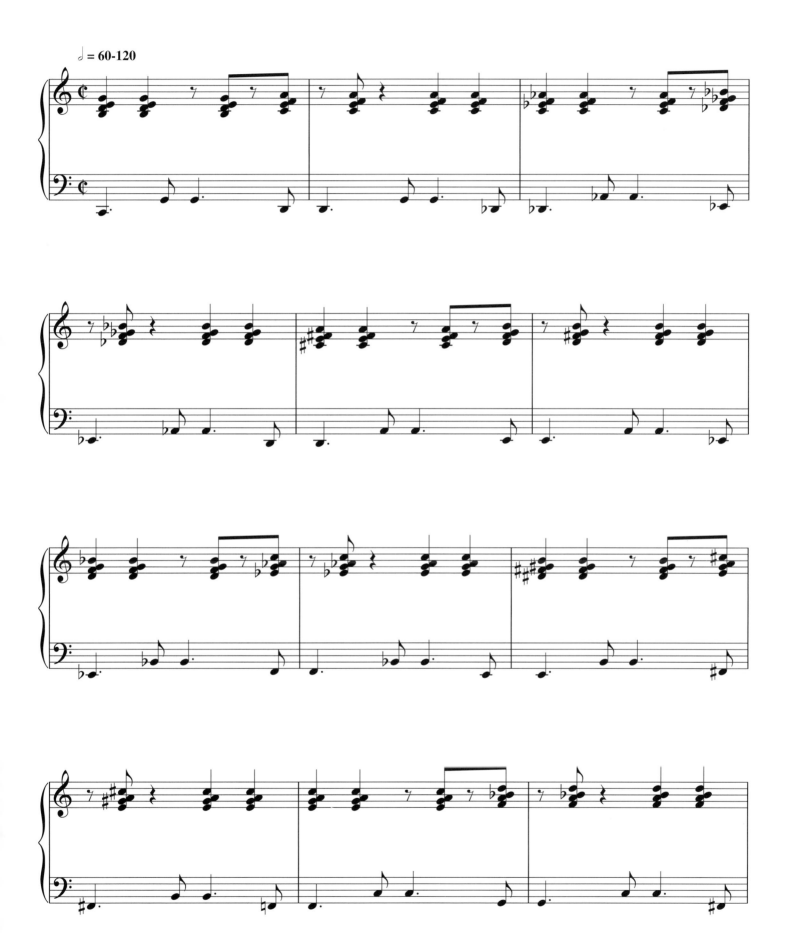

2

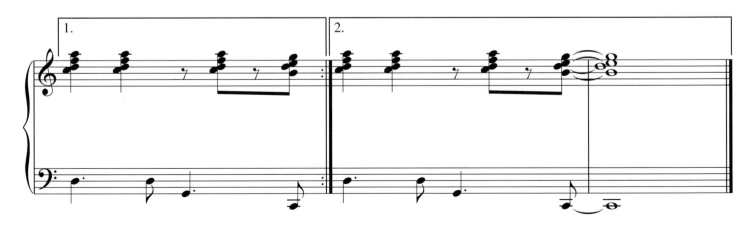

3

4

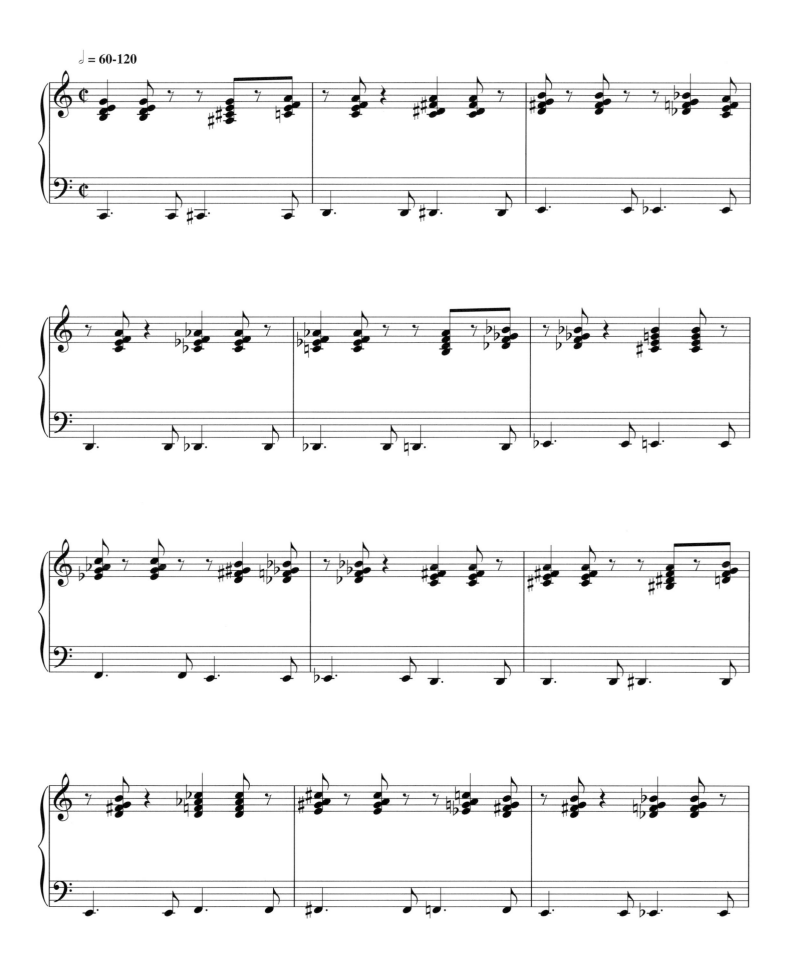

14

5

6

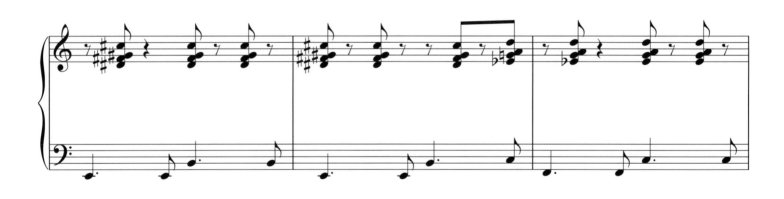

7

8

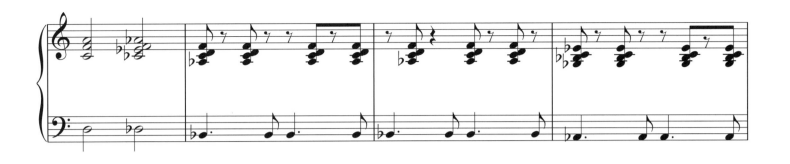

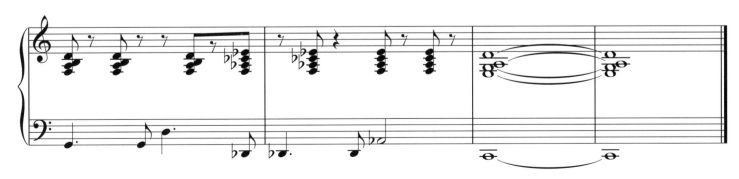

9

10

11

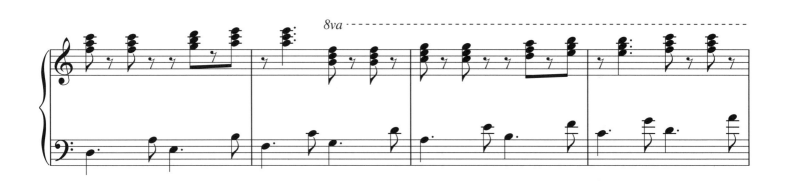

12

13

loco

14

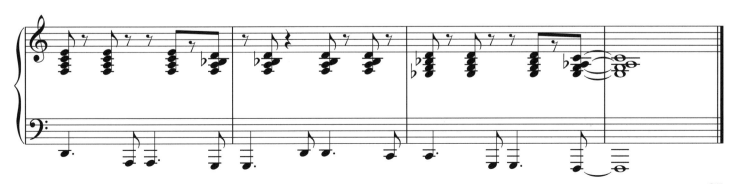

15

𝅗𝅥 = **60-120**

Both hands 8vb

16

17

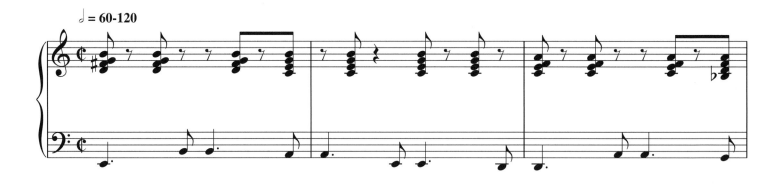

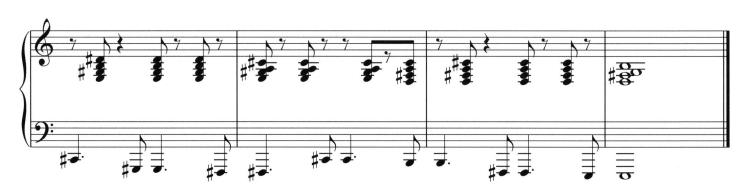

18

19

20

21

22

23

24

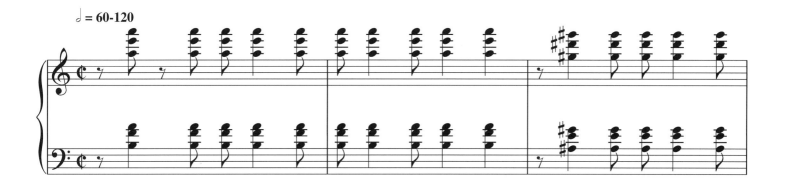

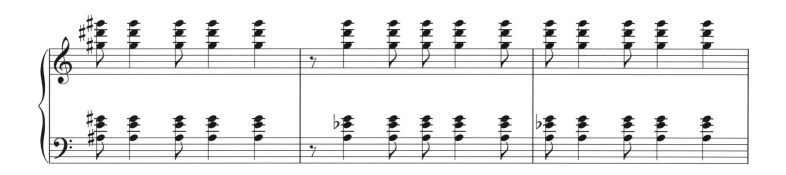

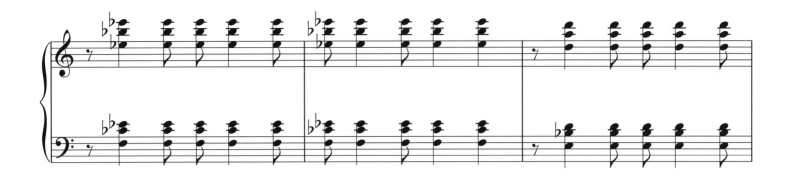

25

26

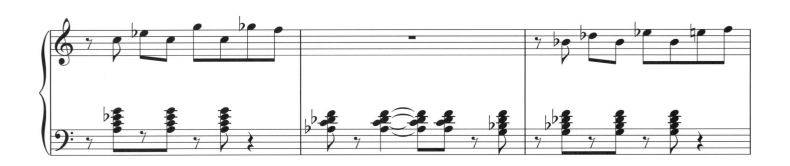

27

28

29

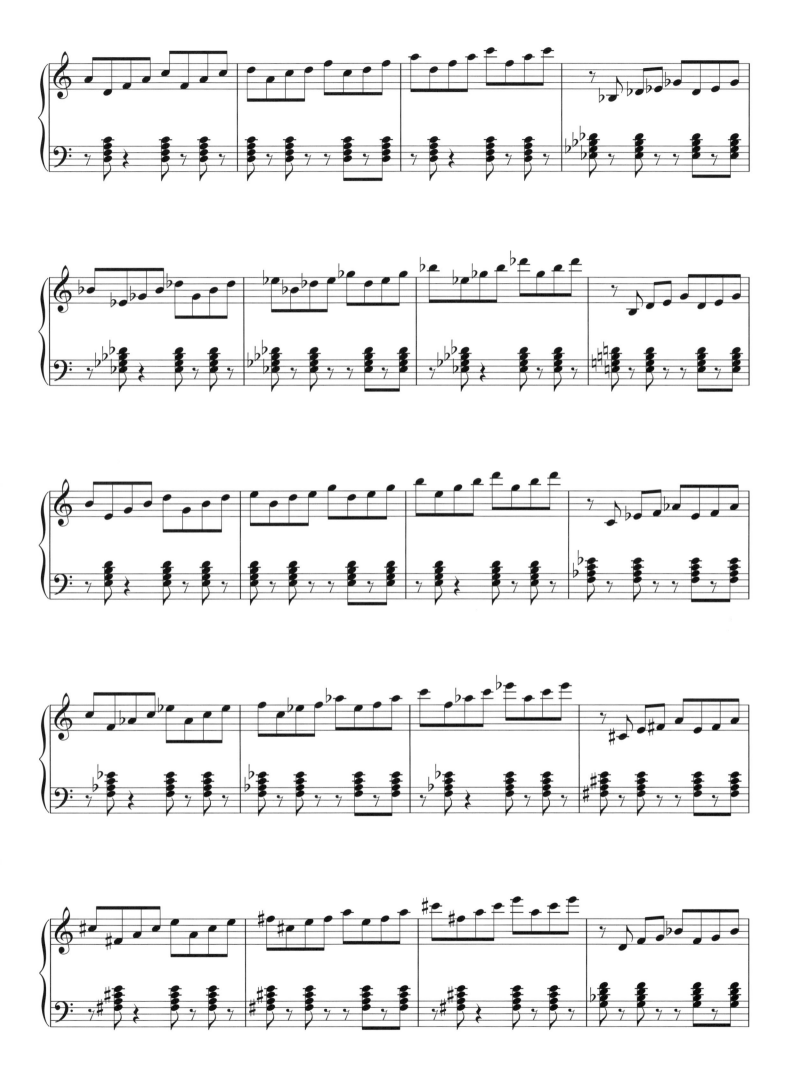

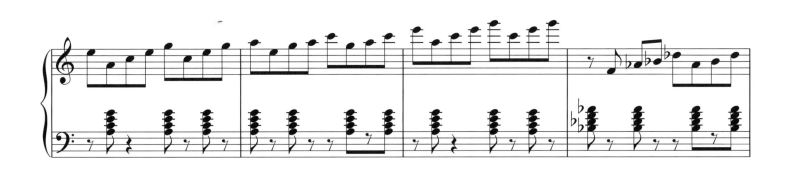

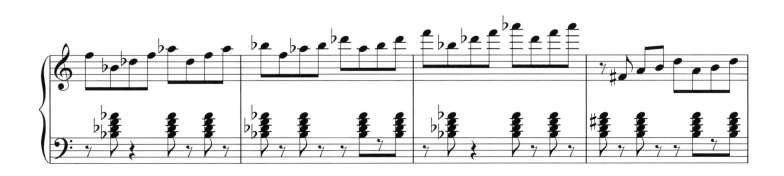

30

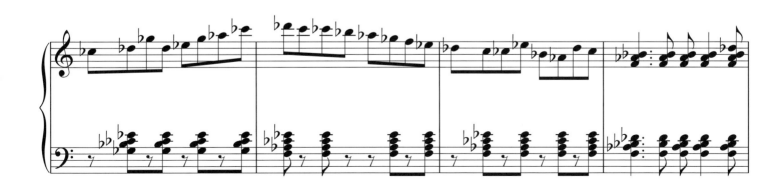

31

32

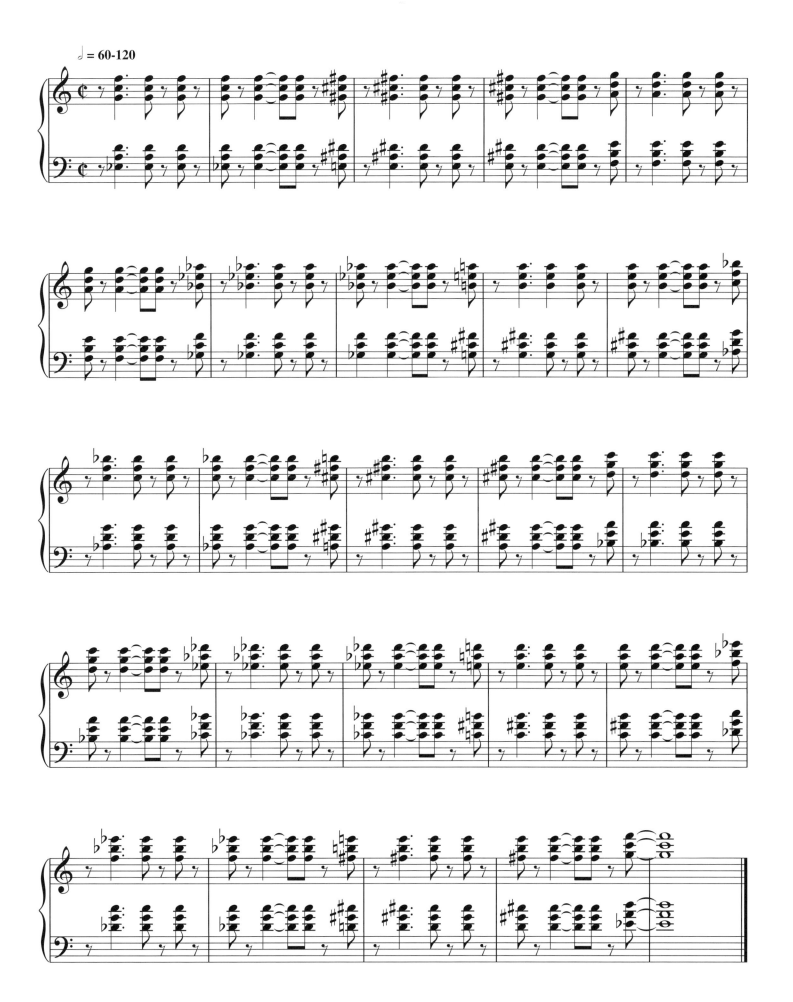

33

34

35

36

37

38

39

40

41

42

43

44

45

46

47

48

49

50

Musicians Institute Press

is the official series of Southern California's renowned music school, Musicians Institute. **MI** instructors, some of the finest musicians in the world, share their vast knowledge and experience with you – no matter what your current level. For guitar, bass, drums, vocals, and keyboards, **MI Press** offers the finest music curriculum for higher learning through a variety of series:

ESSENTIAL CONCEPTS
Designed from MI core curriculum programs.

MASTER CLASS
Designed from MI elective courses.

PRIVATE LESSONS
Tackle a variety of topics "one-on-one" with MI faculty instructors.

KEYBOARD

Blues Hanon
by Peter Deneff • Private Lessons
00695708 .... $14.95

Dictionary of Keyboard Grooves
by Gail Johnson • Private Lessons
00695556 Book/CD Pack $16.95

Funk Keyboards – The Complete Method
by Gail Johnson • Master Class
00695336 Book/CD Pack $14.95

Jazz Chord Hanon
by Peter Deneff • Private Lessons
00695791 .... $12.95

Jazz Hanon
by Peter Deneff • Private Lessons
00695554 .... $12.95

Jazz Piano
by Christian Klikovits • Essential Concepts
00695773 Book/CD Pack $17.95

Keyboard Technique
by Steve Weingard • Essential Concepts
00695365 .... $12.95

Keyboard Voicings
by Kevin King • Essential Concepts
00695209 .... $12.95

Music Reading for Keyboard
by Larry Steelman • Essential Concepts
00695205 .... $12.95

Pop Rock Keyboards
by Henry Sol-Eh Brewer & David Garfield • Private Lessons
00695509 Book/CD Pack $19.95

R&B Soul Keyboards
by Henry J. Brewer • Private Lessons
00695327 Book/CD Pack $16.95

Rock Hanon
by Peter Deneff • Private Lessons
00695784 .... $12.95

Salsa Hanon
by Peter Deneff • Private Lessons
00695226 .... $12.95

Stride Hanon
by Peter Deneff • Private Lessons
00695882 .... $12.95

DRUM

Afro-Cuban Coordination for Drumset
by Maria Martinez • Private Lessons
00695328 Book/CD Pack $14.95

Blues Drumming
by Ed Roscetti • Essential Concepts
00695623 Book/CD Pack $14.95

Brazilian Coordination for Drumset
by Maria Martinez • Master Class
00695284 Book/CD Pack $14.95

Chart Reading Workbook for Drummers
by Bobby Gabriele • Private Lessons
00695129 Book/CD Pack $14.95

Double Bass Drumming
by Jeff Bowders
00695723 Book/CD Pack $19.95

Drummer's Guide to Odd Meters
by Ed Roscetti • Essential Concepts
00695349 Book/CD Pack $14.95

Funk & Hip-Hop Grooves for Drums
by Ed Roscetti • Private Lessons
00695679 Book/CD Pack $14.95

Latin Soloing for Drumset
by Phil Maturano • Private Lessons
00695287 Book/CD Pack $14.95

Musician's Guide to Recording Drums
by Dallan Beck • Master Class
00695755 Book/CD Pack $19.95

Rock Drumming Workbook
by Ed Roscetti • Private Lessons
00695838 Book/CD Pack $19.95

Working the Inner Clock for Drumset
by Phil Maturano • Private Lessons
00695127 Book/CD Pack $16.95

VOICE

Harmony Vocals
by Mike Campbell & Tracee Lewis • Private Lessons
00695262 Book/CD Pack $17.95

Musician's Guide to Recording Vocals
by Dallan Beck • Private Lessons
00695626 Book/CD Pack $14.95

Sightsinging
by Mike Campbell • Essential Concepts
00695195 .... $17.95

Vocal Technique
by Dena Murray • Essential Concepts
00695427 Book/CD Pack $22.95

OTHER REFERENCE

Approach to Jazz Improvisation
by Dave Pozzi • Private Lessons
00695135 Book/CD Pack $17.95

Ear Training
by Keith Wyatt, Carl Schroeder & Joe Elliott • **Essential Concepts**
00695198 Book/2-CD Pack $19.95

Encyclopedia of Reading Rhythms
by Gary Hess • Private Lessons
00695145 .... $19.95

Going Pro
by Kenny Kerner • Private Lessons
00695322 .... $17.95

Harmony & Theory
by Keith Wyatt & Carl Schroeder • Essential Concepts
00695161 .... $17.95

Home Recording Basics
featuring Dallan Beck
00695655 VHS Video $19.95

Lead Sheet Bible
by Robin Randall & Janice Peterson • Private Lessons
00695130 Book/CD Pack $19.95

FOR MORE INFORMATION, SEE YOUR LOCAL MUSIC DEALER,
OR WRITE TO:

HAL•LEONARD® CORPORATION
7777 W. BLUEMOUND RD. P.O. BOX 13819 MILWAUKEE, WI 53213

Visit Hal Leonard Online at **www.halleonard.com**

Prices, contents, and availability subject to change without notice